An Annotated Bibliography

of

The United States Marine Corps'

Concept of Close Air Support

by

James S. Santelli

Historical Branch, G-3 Division

Headquarters, U. S. Marine Corps

Washington, D. C. 20380

1968

DEPARTMENT OF THE NAVY
HEADQUARTERS UNITED STATES MARINE CORPS
WASHINGTON, D. C. 20380

PREFACE

This bibliography is published for the information of all who are interested in the history of the Marine Corps concept of close air support.   Inclusion of a particular work does not necessarily constitute Marine Corps endorsement of that work.

R. G. OWENS, JR.
Major General, U. S. Marine Corps
Assistant Chief of Staff, G-3

Reviewed and Approved: 9 October 1968

AN ANNOTATED BIBLIOGRAPHY OF THE UNITED STATES MARINE CORPS CONCEPT OF CLOSE AIR SUPPORT

Compiled by

JAMES S. SANTELLI

Introduction

The list which follows consists of publications dealing in whole or in part with the development and employment of close air support by the Marine Corps. The scope of the bibliography covers a period of time which begins with the first real combat employment of the technique of close air support in Nicaragua in 1927 through the war in Vietnam.

To obtain the greatest possible value to the largest number of researchers and writers, broad criteria for selection of items to be included have been utilized. Inclusion of any given title does not, therefore, constitute Marine Corps acceptance or endorsement of an author's views, conclusions, or indeed, complete historical accuracy. By the same token, the annotation supplied is in the nature of description of the contents of books and articles rather than a critical evaluation.

The abbreviation "CAS" denotes the phrase "close air support." The annotation "notes" indicates that the publication is documented as to research sources; "bibliog." indicates that a bibliography of research materials is appended. The inclusion of illustrations is indicated by "illus."

GENERAL

1. BGen Norman J. Anderson, USMC. "Marine Aviation Ready for any Emergency: Air-Ground Team Concept Value is Hailed." Army Navy Air Force Journal and Register, v. 100, no. 10 (3 Nov 1962), pp. 18-19.

   A brief description of the role of Marine aviation in the air-ground team concept.

2. Capt Robert B. Asprey, USMC. "Close Air Support." Army, v. 12, no. 4 (Nov 1961), pp. 33-37. illus.

   An argument for the adoption by the Army of a sounder doctrine of CAS with praise for the Marine concept of the doctrine.

3. Maj W. H. Beckett, USMC. "The L2VMA Light CAS Needs Boondockers." Marine Corps Gazette, v. 47, no. 3 (Mar 1963), pp. 20-23. illus.

   The author extols the virtues and advantages of a proposed light attack aircraft (L2VMA) for use in counterinsurgency.

4. ----------------------. "Our Growing CAS Gap." Marine Corps Gazette, v. 48, no. 4 (Apr 1964), pp. 47-48.

   A presentation of the author's views on the type of aircraft that is needed in CAS missions.

5. MajGen Arthur F. Binney, USMC. "Marine Aviation--a Partner." Army Information Digest, v. 16, no. 7 (Jul 1961), pp. 74-79.

   A brief historical account of Marine aviation with only a few references on the doctrine of CAS.

6. LtCol J. F. Bolt, USMC. "Goodbye Able Dog." Marine Corps Gazette, v. 41, no. 10 (Oct 1957), pp. 28-31. illus.

   This article enumerates the advantages and disadvantages of replacing the Douglas "Skyraider" (AD) with the Douglas "Skyhawk" (A4D) aircraft in regards to its use in CAS.

7. Maj Harvey D. Bradshaw, USMC. "Marine Corps Aviation: Cunningham to Chu Lai." United States Naval Institute Proceedings, v. 92, no. 11 (Nov 1966), pp. 106-123. illus.

    A pictorial history of Marine aviation with some reference to the development of CAS.

8. Sgt F. R. Burke, USMC. "On Target, Courtesy of MASS-3," Naval Aviation News (Nov 1958), pp. 38-39. illus.

    A brief explanation of directing aircraft to a target in air support missions.

9. "Close Air Support." The Officer, v. 33, no. 6 (Jun 1957), pp. 14-15, +. illus.

    Differing views on CAS as expressed by the Air Force and the Marine Corps.

10. Maj Alfred Drago, USMC. "The High Price of Air Control." Marine Corps Gazette, v. 48, no. 3 (Mar 1964), pp. 30-31. illus.

    The article outlines the duties of a forward air controller and proposes the substitution of enlisted Marines for Naval Aviators as forward air controllers.

11. Ernest F. Fisher, Jr., and Richard P. Wienert. "Combat Data Concerning the Effectiveness of Close Air Support." Manuscript. Washington: Office of the Chief of Military History, Department of the Army, n. d., 156 pp.

    This study is an attempt to provide a reasonably accurate body of data on the effectiveness of CAS in WW II and Korea from which certain conclusions can be derived.

12. LtCol Delbert M. Fowler, USA. "Close Air Support." The Military Engineer, v. 52, no. 350 (Nov--Dec 1960), pp. 461-462.

    The author advocates the incorporation of Marine Corps concepts in the Army's doctrine of CAS.

13. LtCol T. N. Greene, USMC. "Support by Fire (part III)
    Close Air Support: Quo Vadis?" <u>Marine Corps
    Gazette</u>, v. 43, no. 9 (Sep 1959), pp. 38-42. illus.

       Presentation of certain recommendations by the
    author to aid in making CAS more effective.

14. Col Robert D. Heinl, Jr., USMC. <u>Soldiers of the Sea</u>.
    Annapolis, Md: United States Naval Institute, 1962.
    692 pp. illus, maps, appendices.

       Contains brief references to the development
    of CAS in the Marine Corps.

15. LtCol R. P. Keller, USMC. "Trained for Support." <u>Marine
    Corps Gazette</u>, v. 38, no. 5 (May 1954), pp. 28-31.
    illus.

       A concise discussion of aviation training in
    the Marine Corps.

16. LtCol G. C. McClure, USMC. "Take Cover in the Air."
    <u>Marine Corps Gazette</u>, v. 46, no. 4 (Apr 1962),
    pp. 52-53.

       Some general thinking on the use of CAS.

17. Capt D. C. MacMichael, USMC. "Bottleneck in Close Air
    Support." <u>Marine Corps Gazette</u>, v. 43, no. 5
    (May 1959), pp. 38-39.

       The author considers the necessity of modifying
    the methods used in CAS in accordance with nuclear
    age tactics.

18. "Marine Aviation--It Provides Air Support for the Corps
    Ground Forces." <u>Navy, The Magazine of Sea Power</u>,
    v. 7, no. 6 (Jun 1964), pp. 20-23, illus.

       A general look at the mission of Marine
    aviation with some references to CAS.

19. Maj Bruce J. Matheson, USMC. "Round-the-Clock Close Air
         Support." <u>Marine Corps Gazette</u>, v. 38, no. 9
         (Sep 1954), pp. 12-15. illus.

         This article focuses attention on the develop-
     ment of night CAS while at the same time advocating
     the extended use of it.

20. MajGen Vernon E. Megee, USMC. "Tactical Air Support of
         Ground Forces." <u>Marine Corps Gazette</u>, v. 39, no. 12
         (Dec 1955), pp. 12-17. illus.

         The author, a veteran Marine pilot, describes
     the procedures that are necessary for the proper co-
     ordination of air and ground units and the intricacies
     involved in the execution of the tactics of CAS.

21. LtCol Allen G. Pixton, USA. "Close Air Support in
         Amphibious Operations." <u>Military Review</u>, v. 23,
         no. 5 (Aug 1953), pp. 27-34. illus.

         An examination of the differences in the CAS
     systems as utilized by the different services.

22. Robert Sherrod. "Marine Corps Aviation: The Early Days."
         <u>Marine Corps Gazette</u>, v. 36, no. 6 (Jun 1952),
         pp. 52-61. illus.

         A historical account of Marine aviation from
     World War I to World War II with only minor
     reference to the development of CAS.

23. "The Story of Marine Aviation." <u>Navy, The Magazine of
     Sea Power</u>, v. 8, no. 7 (Jul 1965), p. 21, +.

         Contains a brief look at the growth of CAS.

24. TSgt Robert W. Tallent, USMC. "Aviation Birthday."
         <u>Leatherneck</u>, v. 35, no. 6 (Jun 1952), pp. 16-23,
         +. illus.

         This article includes a brief look at the develop-
     ment of CAS in the Marine Corps.

25. Joel D. Thacker. "Wings of the Marine Corps." *Marine Corps Gazette*, v. 27, no. 4 (Aug 1943), pp. 29-32. illus.

    A discussion of the different types of aircraft that were used by the Marine Corps between 1914 and 1943.

26. LtCol Marshall R. Tutton, USMC. "Marine Corps Aviation." *United States Naval Institute Proceedings*, v. 87, no. 5 (May 1961), pp. 48-53. illus.

    Includes a discussion of innovations in the air-ground team concept during the post-Korean War years.

27. U. S. Department of the Navy. Office of the Chief of Naval Operations. *Naval Aviation in Review*. Washington: Government Printing Office, 1958. 388 pp. illus.

    A record of the history and development of Naval aviation, including a brief synopsis on the history of Marine aviation with references to the growth of CAS in the Marine Corps.

28. U. S. Marine Corps. *Air Support*, FMFM 7-3, Quantico, Virginia, 1966. 92 pp. maps, charts.

    The fundamentals and classification of air support operations and the planning, execution, air intelligence, and logistical considerations in the conduct of air operations are discussed. Also included is a chapter on the definition and the mission of CAS.

29. Capt J. M. Verdi, USMCR. "The Case for Jet CAS." *Marine Corps Gazette*, v. 45, no. 6 (Jun 1961), pp. 32-35, illus.

    A review and comparison of jet versus conventional aircraft performance in CAS missions.

30. Maj J. M. Verdi, USMC. "Light VMA: A Better Answer." Marine Corps Gazette, v. 48, no. 2 (Feb 1964), pp. 27-29.

> Recommendations by the author that an attack aircraft meet certain specific requirements before it is used in air support missions.

31. Maj Hal Vincent, USMC. "Moonlighting." Marine Corps Gazette, v. 46, no. 7 (Jul 1962), pp. 31-33. illus.

> This article examines some of the techniques that are used in night CAS.

32. Capt W. F. Wagner, USMC. "Air--Suppress that Incoming." Marine Corps Gazette, v. 39, no. 5 (May 1955), pp. 18-20. illus.

> This article advocates the greater use of air support for ground forces.

33. Capt R. K. Wood, USMC. "Night CAS." Marine Corps Gazette, v. 46, no. 7 (Jul 1962), pp. 27-30. illus.

> A proposal that the Marine Corps increase the emphasis placed on night CAS.

NICARAGUA

34. Capt Charles W. Boggs, Jr., USMC. "Marine Aviation: Origin and Growth." Marine Corps Gazette, v. 34, no. 11 (Nov 1950), pp. 68-75. illus.

> Some references to the development of the doctrine of CAS during the 1920s.

35. Maj E. H. Brainard, USMC. "Marine Corps Aviation." Marine Corps Gazette, v. 13, no. 1 (Mar 1928), pp. 25-26.

> This article takes into account the development of air/ground communications in jungle areas while providing a contemporary graphic description of the first use of dive-bombing in combat over Ocotal, Nicaragua.

36. Capt H. Denny Campbell, USMC. "Aviation in Guerrilla Warfare." Marine Corps Gazette, v. 15, no. 5 (May 1931), pp. 35-42; v. 16, no. 3 (Nov 1931), pp. 33-40.

   Views by the author on the possible and potential employment of air power in bush warfare and the advantages that can be derived from its use.

37. Midn William Roland Glover, USN. "Close Air Support as Developed by the United States in Nicaragua, 1927-1933." Midshipman Essays Class of 1954. Annapolis, Maryland: United States Naval Institute, 1955, pp. 19-30. bibliog.

   An account of the development and the initial beginnings of the Marine air/ground team concept.

38. "Marine Aviation, a Record of Achievement." Marine Corps Gazette, v. 15, no. 3 (Nov 1930), pp. 33-41. illus.

   A history of early Marine Corps aviation with some mention of the development of air support.

39. "Marine Aviators in Nicaragua." Leatherneck, v. 11, no. 3 (Mar 1928), p. 25.

   Reprint of part of the weekly operations of Marine Observation Squadron Seven (VO-7M) with reference to support of ground forces.

40. Gen Vernon E. Megee, USMC (Ret). "The Evolution of Marine Aviation," Part 1. Marine Corps Gazette, v. 49, no. 8 (Aug 1965), pp. 20-26. illus.

   A history of Marine aviation to the outbreak of World War II along with some remarks on the development of CAS.

41. --------------------------------. "The Genesis of Air Support in Guerrilla Operations." United States Naval Institute Proceedings, v. 91, no. 6 (Jun 1965), pp. 48-59. illus. map.

   A description of the growth of CAS in Nicaragua with recommendations by the author of what is needed in Vietnam to make the doctrine more effective there.

42. Capt Francis E. Pierce, USMC. "Infantry-Air Communication." Marine Corps Gazette, v. 13, no. 4 (Dec 1938), pp. 266-270.

    A look at the methods utilized in accomplishing liaison between ground troops and supporting aircraft as envisioned during the late 1920s.

43. Maj Ross E. Rowell, USMC. "Aircraft in Bush Warfare." Marine Corps Gazette, v. 14, no. 3 (Sep 1929), pp. 180-203.

    A very detailed treatise on Marine aviation in Nicaragua with a considerable amount of attention paid to the development of air-ground communications and the use of aircraft against enemy personnel.

44. ------------------------. "The Air Service in Minor Warfare." United States Naval Institute Proceedings, v. 55, no. 10 (Oct 1929), pp. 871-877.

    A description of the first use of dive-bombing.

45. ------------------------. "Annual Report of Aircraft Squadrons, Second Brigade, U. S. Marine Corps, July 1, 1927, to June 20, 1928." Marine Corps Gazette, v. 13, no. 4 (Dec 1928), pp. 248-265. illus.

    A general consideration of the various usages of Marine aircraft in Nicaragua with specific references to the intercommunication between the air and ground patrols and the use of air attacks directed by ground troops.

46. U. S. Marine Corps. Marine Corps Aviation, General, 1940. Washington: Government Printing Office, 1940. 70 pp.

    A booklet setting forth pre-World War II thinking on the mission, organization, characteristics, and tactical employment of Marine Corps aviation.

47. U. S. Marine Corps. <u>Small</u> <u>Wars</u> <u>Manual</u>: <u>United</u> <u>States</u>
    <u>Marine</u> <u>Corps</u> <u>1940</u>. Washington: Government Printing
    Office, 1940. Ch 9, pp. 1-24.

    Chapter Nine, "Aviation" reflects pre-World
    War II thinking on the use of Marine aviation in
    small wars with some discussion on the employment
    of air support for ground troops.

48. ------------------. <u>A</u> <u>Text</u> <u>on</u> <u>the</u> <u>Employment</u> <u>of</u> <u>Marine</u>
    <u>Corps</u> <u>Aviation</u>. Quantico, Virginia: Marine Corps
    Schools, 1935. 84 pp.

    The document is indicative of the thinking of
    the Marine Corps in the mid-1930s as to the tactical
    employment of Marine aviation in landing operations
    and small wars.

WORLD WAR II

49. "Air Support of Ground Units." <u>Marine</u> <u>Corps</u> <u>Gazette</u>,
    v. 27, no. 6 (Oct 1943), p. 48.

    A definition of tactics as used in early air
    support operations against the Japanese.

50. Board to Reexamine the Adequacy of Present Concept of
    Mission and Functions of the Marine Corps. <u>An</u>
    <u>Evaluation</u> <u>of</u> <u>Air</u> <u>Operations</u> <u>Affecting</u> <u>the</u> <u>U.</u> <u>S.</u>
    <u>Marine</u> <u>Corps</u> <u>in</u> <u>World</u> <u>War</u> <u>II</u>. Quantico, Virginia:
    Marine Corps Schools, 1945. var. pg. maps, charts.

    An evaluation of air operations affecting the
    Marine Corps during the war with Japan with a de-
    tailed exposition of the Marine doctrine and tech-
    nique of CAS as developed in World War II.

51. Maj Charles W. Boggs, Jr., USMC. <u>Marine</u> <u>Aviation</u> <u>in</u> <u>the</u>
    <u>Philippines</u>. Washington: Historical Division,
    Headquarters, U. S. Marine Corps, 1951. 166 pp.
    illus., maps, appendices.

    An account of the use of air support for ground
    forces in the campaign along with a brief summary of
    the development of CAS in World War II.

9

52. Sgt Don Braman, USMC. "Cannonball Support." <u>Leatherneck</u>, v. 28, no. 10 (Oct 1945), pp. 30-32. illus.

   A brief account of the use of air support on Okinawa.

53. Wesley F. Craven and James L. Cate, eds. <u>The Pacific: Guadalcanal to Saipan, August 1942 to July 1944---The Army Air Forces in World War II</u>. v. 4. Chicago: University of Chicago Press, 1953. 693 pp. illus., maps, notes.

   Army aviation in support of operations from Guadalcanal to the Marianas, with only minor references on the use of Marine aviation.

54. --. <u>The Pacific: Matterhorn to Nagasaki, June 1944 to August 1945--- The Army Air Forces in World War II</u>. v. 5. Chicago: University of Chicago Press, 1953. 878 pp.

   Contains some mention of Marine aviation as utilized in the Philippines and at Ulithi.

55. Capt John A. DeChant, USMCR. <u>Devilbirds: The Story of United States Marine Corps Aviation in World War II</u>. New York: Harper & Brothers Publishers, 1947. 265 pp. illus.

   A general chronicle of the activities of Marine aviation in World War II with emphasis on offensive air operations.

56. Capt Warren H. Goodman, USMC. "One Job--One Corps." <u>Marine Corps Gazette</u>, v. 28, no. 11 (Nov 1944), pp. 22-24. illus.

   An outline of the mission of Marine aviation in regards to its support of ground troops.

57. Maj Carl W. Hoffman, USMC. <u>Saipan: The Beginning of the End</u>. Washington: Historical Division, Headquarters, U. S. Marine Corps, 1950. 286 pp. illus., maps, appendices, bibliog.

   Included in this volume is an evaluation of the use of air power against the enemy.

58. Maj Carl W. Hoffman, USMC. The Seizure of Tinian.
    Washington: Historical Division, Headquarters,
    U. S. Marine Corps, 1951. 169 pp. illus., maps,
    appendices, bibliog.

        This work, although it contains no major
    'references on the subject, does point out that
    Tinian saw the first extensive combat use of napalm.

59. Maj Frank O. Hough, USMCR. The Assault on Peleliu.
    Washington: Historical Division, Headquarters,
    U. S. Marine Corps, 1950. 209 pp. illus., maps,
    appendices, bibliog.

        A brief narrative on the employment of aviation
    is enclosed in the appendices.

60. LtCol-----------------------and Maj John A. Crown, USMCR,
    The Campaign on New Britain. Washington: Historical
    Branch, G-3 Division, Headquarters, U. S. Marine Corps,
    1952. 220 pp. illus., maps, appendices, bibliog.

        Only very little mention on the use of air
    power in the battle.

61. ----------------------------, Maj Verle E. Ludwig, USMC,
    and Henry I. Shaw, Jr. Pearl Harbor to Guadalcanal
    ---History of U. S. Marine Corps Operations in World
    War II, v. 1. Washington: Historical Branch, G-3
    Division, Headquarters, U. S. Marine Corps, 1958.
    449 pp. illus., maps, notes, bibliog.

        Operations of Marine Corps units in the early
    phases of World War II. Although containing very
    little mention of CAS this work is useful in acquiring
    background knowledge for the later application and
    development of the theory during the war.

62. Maj O. R. Lodge, USMC. The Recapture of Guam. Washington:
    Historical Branch, G-3 Division, Headquarters, U. S.
    Marine Corps, 1954. 214 pp. illus., maps, appendices,
    bibliog.

        Includes some comments on the use of air support
    during the operation.

63. LtCol Keith B. McCutcheon, USMC. "Close Air Support on Luzon." Marine Corps Gazette, v. 29, no. 9 (Sep 1945), pp. 38-39.

A short account of MAG-24's participation in the Luzon Campaign in support of the U. S. Army's 1st Cavalry Division.

64. -------------------------------. "Close Air Support SOP." Marine Corps Gazette, v. 29, no. 8 (Aug 1945), pp. 48-50.

A look at what was considered necessary for the effective utilization of CAS during World War II.

65. Gen Vernon E. Megee, USMC (Ret). "The Evolution of Marine Aviation," Part II. Marine Corps Gazette, v. 49, no. 9 (Sep 1965), pp. 55-60.

Traces the history of Marine aviation in World War II.

66. Capt John McJennet, USMC. "Air Power for Infantry." Marine Corps Gazette, v. 29, no. 8 (Aug 1945), pp. 15-16, +. illus.

A record of the use of CAS in the Pacific.

67. John Miller, Jr. Cartwheel: The Reduction of Rabaul--- The War in the Pacific---United States Army in World War II. Washington: Office of the Chief of Military History, Department of the Army, 1959. 418 pp. illus., maps, notes, bibliog.

Contains considerable material on Marines in the New Georgia and Bougainville operations with a few remarks on Marine aviation.

68. ---------------, Guadalcanal: The First Offensive---The War in the Pacific---United States Army in World War II. Washington: Office of the Chief of Military History, Department of the Army, 1949. 413 pp. illus., maps, notes, bibliog.

Only brief references to Marine aviation on Guadalcanal.

69. Robert C. Miller. "Air Power in the Solomons." Marine
    Corps Gazette, v. 27, no. 1 (Mar-Apr 1943), pp. 45-50.

        A report on the use of aviation during the
    first phase of the Guadalcanal campaign.

70. Maj Charles S. Nichols, Jr., USMC and Henry I. Shaw, Jr.
    Okinawa: Victory in the Pacific. Washington:
    Historical Branch, G-3 Division, Headquarters, U. S.
    Marine Corps, 1955. 332 pp. illus., maps, appendices.

        Includes some remarks on the use of air support.

71. Maj John N. Rentz, USMCR. Bougainville and the Northern
    Solomons. Washington: Historical Section, Division
    of Information, Headquarters, U. S. Marine Corps,
    1948. 166 pp. illus., maps, appendices.

        Contains some brief statements on the use of
    air support.

72. -----------------------. "Marine Corps Aviation--An
    Infantryman's Opinion." United States Naval Institute
    Proceedings, v. 75, no. 11 (Nov 1949), pp. 1276-
    1269. illus.

        An explanation and definition of the CAS doctrine
    as practiced by the Marine Corps.

73. -----------------------. Marines in the Central Solomons.
    Washington: Historical Branch, G-3 Division, Head-
    quarters, U. S. Marine Corps, 1952. 186 pp. illus.,
    maps, appendices, bibliog.

        Contains some scattered references to the use of
    air power during the campaign, but more important
    this volume points out that the modern Marine Corps
    technique of CAS had its beginning in this engagement.

74. Henry I. Shaw, Jr., Bernard C. Nalty, and Edwin T.
        Turnbladh. *Central Pacific Drive---History of U. S.
        Marine Corps Operations in World War II*, v. 3.
        Washington: Historical Branch, G-3 Division,
        Headquarters, U. S. Marine Corps, 1966. 695 pp.
        illus., maps, notes, bibliog.

        The following Marine operations are covered in
        this volume: the Gilberts, the Marshalls, Saipan,
        and Guam. It also encompasses some commentary on
        the employment of aviation.

75. ------------------, and Maj Douglas T. Kane, UMSC.
        *Isolation of Rabaul---History of the U. S. Marine
        Corps Operations in World War II*, v. 2. Washington:
        Historical Branch, G-3 Division, Headquarters, U. S.
        Marine Corps, 1963. 633 pp. illus., maps, notes,
        bibliog.

        A detailed narrative of Marine campaigns in the
        Pacific from Feb 1943 to Jun 1944 with considerable
        attention given to the use of aviation.

76. Robert Sherrod. *History of Marine Corps Aviation in
        World War II*. Washington: Combat Forces Press,
        1952. 496 pp. illus., charts, maps, appendices.

        A comprehensive and detailed study of Marine
        aviation in World War II with a look at the develop-
        ment and evolution of CAS during the war. The work
        also contains a brief background sketch of the early
        period of aviation in the Marine Corps.

77. Robert Ross Smith. *Triumph in the Philippines---The War
        in the Pacific---United States Army in World War II*.
        Washington: Office of the Chief of Military History,
        Department of the Army, 1963. 765 pp. illus., maps,
        notes, bibliog.

        Includes a number of remarks on the participation
        of Marine aviation in the liberation of the Philippines,
        1944-1945.

78. Capt Donald A. Stauffer, USMC. "Marine Aviation at Peleliu."
        Marine Corps Gazette, v. 29, no. 2 (Feb 1945),
        pp. 17-19. illus.

        Includes a discussion on air support for ground
        forces.

14

79. Maj W. E. Sullivan, Jr., USMC. "History and Development of Close Air Support." *Marine Corps Gazette*, v. 40, no. 11 (Nov 1956), pp. 20-24. illus.

　　Primarily deals with the use of the doctrine in World War II, and to a lesser degree in Korea.

80. Maj W. G. Wethe, USMC. "Marine Aviation in Support of Amphibious Troops." *Marine Corps Gazette*, v. 35, no. 1 (Jan 1951), pp. 26-35. illus.

　　A critical evaluation of the use of CAS on Okinawa with a discussion on the lessons learned from World War II and how they can be applied to make the CAS doctrine more effective.

81. Maj John L. Zimmerman, USMCR. *The Guadalcanal Campaign*. Washington: Historical Division, Headquarters, U. S. Marine Corps, 1949. 189 pp. illus., maps, appendices, bibliog.

　　Incorporated within this work is an examination of the operations of the 1st and 2d Marine Aircraft Wings on Guadalcanal in the Solomons, 7 Aug 1942-9 Feb 1943.

KOREA

82. "A Chronology of Marine Corps Aviation in Korea." *Leatherneck*, v. 39, no. 11 (Nov 1956), pp. 47-50, +. illus.

　　A short, general chronology covering the period from 5 Jul 1950 to 27 Jul 1953.

83. "Air Power in Korea--Ground Support." *United States Naval Institute Proceedings*, v. 78, no. 2 (Feb 1952), pp. 221-222.

　　Brief comments on the controversy over CAS as practiced by the Marine Corps in Korea.

84. Col Charles L. Banks, USMC, and Col Jack R. Cram, USMC. "Win Place and Show for the Jets." Marine Corps Gazette, v. 35, no. 12 (Dec 1951), pp. 15-17. illus.

A two-way approach to the problem of CAS, giving the views of the pilot and the ground officer, with examples from the Korean War.

85. Charles L. Black. "The Truth About Air Support." Flying, v. 48, no. 2 (Feb 1951), pp. 11-15, +. illus.

Comparison of CAS as practiced by the different branches of the services during the first months of fighting in Korea.

86. LtCol J. F. Bolt, USMC. "Point Blank Bombing." Marine Corps Gazette, v. 41, no. 8 (Aug 1957), pp. 10-13. illus.

Recommendation by the author for more acceptance of point-blank bombing as was devised and used in Korea.

87. MSgt Fred G. Braitsch, Jr., USMC. "Air Strike." Leatherneck, v. 36, no. 4 (Apr 1953), p. 16-20. illus.

Depiction of a Marine air strike in support of ground operation demonstrating the interplay of forward air controllers, the air and ground units, and the Tactical Air Direction Center.

88. ---------------------------------. "Checkerboard Squadron." Leatherneck, v. 35, no. 10 (Oct 1952), pp. 40-47. illus.

The article deals with the operations of Marine Attack Squadron (VMA) 312 in Korea.

89. ---------------------------------. "Flying Sergeants." Leatherneck, v. 35, no. 2 (Feb 1952), pp. 14-19. illus.

Review of the services of Marine enlisted pilots in the war.

90. MSgt Fred G. Braitsch, Jr., USMC. "Marine Air War." *Leatherneck*, v. 34, no. 11 (Nov 1951), pp. 30-35. illus.

   A general summation of the first year of Marine air operations in the war.

91. ----------------------------------. "Marine Air War." *Leatherneck*, v. 35, no. 11 (Nov 1952), pp. 30-35. illus.

   A review of the second year of Marine air operations in the war.

92. ----------------------------------. "Night Intruders." *Leatherneck*, v. 34, no. 12 (Dec 1951), pp. 21-25. illus.

   Marine Night Fighter Squadron (VMF(N)) 513 and the utilization of the Grumman F7F "Tigercats."

93. ----------------------------------. "Skyraiders." *Leatherneck*, v. 35, no. 4 (Apr 1952), pp. 16-21. illus.

   A general look at the missions of Marine Attack Squadron (VMA) 121 and its use of the Douglas AD "Skyraider."

94. "Close Air Support." *Flying*, v. 49, no. 5 (Nov 1951), pp. 56-58, +. illus.

   An examination of the use of this technique by the Marine Corps during the first year of the war with emphasis on the close liaison between the air and ground forces.

95. Kenneth W. Condit and Ernest H. Giusti. "Marine Air at the Chosin Reservoir." *Marine Corps Gazette*, v. 36, no. 7 (Jul 1952). illus., maps.

   Recounts the first major test of the doctrine of CAS in blunting the attack of the Chinese Communists.

96. Kenneth W. Condit and Ernest H. Giusti. "Marine Air Covers the Breakout." Marine Corps Gazette, v. 36, no. 8 (Aug 1952), pp. 20-27. maps.

   Deals with the employment of CAS at the Chosin Reservoir and its value in preventing a total disaster for ground forces.

97. --. "Marine Air Over Inchon-Seoul." Marine Corps Gazette, v. 36, no. 6 (Jun 1952), pp. 18-27. illus., maps.

   A recapitulation of the activities of the 1st Marine Aircraft Wing immediately after the landings at Inchon with numerous references to the furnishing of air support to ground troops.

98. LtCol S. B. Folsom, USMC. "Korea--A Reflection from the Air." United States Naval Institute Proceedings, v. 82, no. 7 (Jul 1956), pp. 732-735. illus.

   A brief, critical evaluation of the effectiveness of air interdiction in the war, especially that of night missions.

99. MSgt Robert T. Fugate, USMC. "Flying Nightmares." Leatherneck, v. 36, no. 8 (Aug 1953), pp. 16-19, +. illus.

   Night operations of Marine Night Fighter Squadron (VMF(N)) 513.

100. Robert Frank Futrell. The United States Air Force in Korea, 1950-1953. New York: Duell, Sloan, and Pearce, 1961. 796 pp. illus., maps, notes, bibliog.

   General history of Air Force operations in the war with many references to Marine Corps aviation.

101. Ernest H. Giusti. "Marine Air Over the Pusan Perimeter." Marine Corps Gazette, v. 36, no. 5 (May 1952), pp. 18-27. illus., maps.

   A discourse on the initial use of CAS by the Marine Corps in Korea.

102. Capt Walter Karig, USNR, Cdr Malcolm W. Cagle, USN, and LCdr Frank A. Manson, USN. Battle Report--The War in Korea. New York: Rinehart, 1952. 520 pp. illus., maps, appendices.

   Primarily, a general account of Navy and Marine Corps operations through the Hungnam evacuation with some discussion on the employment of air support.

103. "Magnificent Support." Leatherneck, v. 34, no. 4 (Apr 1951), pp. 48-49.

   Extracts from a letter of appreciation from Major General Oliver P. Smith, Commanding General, 1st Marine Division, to Major General Field Harris, Commanding General, 1st Marine Aircraft Wing, for the air support given to ground troops in the withdrawal from the Chosin Reservoir.

104. Lynn Montross and Capt Nicholas A. Canzona, USMC. The Chosin Reservoir Campaign---U. S. Marine Operations in Korea, 1950-1953. v. III Washington: Historical Branch, G-3 Division, Headquarters, U. S. Marine Corps, 1957. 432 pp. illus., maps, notes, bibliog.

   A fair amount of attention is paid to the operations of the 1st Marine Aircraft Wing, 26 Oct-24 Dec 1950.

105. --------------, Maj Hubard D. Kuokka, USMC, and Maj Norman W. Hicks, USMC. The East-Central Front---U. S. Marine Operations in Korea, 1950-1953, v. IV. Washington: Historical Branch, G-3 Division, Headquarters, U. S. Marine Corps, 1962. 342 pp. illus., maps, notes, bibliog.

   This volume embraces a great deal of information on the employment of Marine aviation and also the use of CAS, Dec 1950-Mar 1952.

106. ------------- and Capt Nicholas A. Canzona, USMC. The Inchon-Seoul Operation---U. S. Marine Operations in Korea, 1950-1953, v. II. Washington: Historical Branch, G-3 Division, Headquarters, U. S. Marine Corps, 1955. 361 pp. illus., maps, notes, bibliog.

   Includes a chapter on Marine air support at the time of the Inchon landing.

107. Lynn Montross and Capt Nicholas A. Canzona, USMC. The Pusan Perimeter---U. S. Marine Operations in Korea, 1950-1953. v. I. Washington: Historical Branch, G-3 Division, Headquarters, U. S. Marine Corps, 1954. 271 pp. illus., maps, notes, bibliog.

   Includes a number of references on the employment of Marine aviation.

108. "Naval Air Power in Action." Flying, v. 49, no. 5 (Nov 1951), pp. 43-45, +.

   Contains a brief statement on the use of CAS in the opening days of the war.

109. LtCol C. A. Phillips, USMC (Ret), and Maj H. D. Kuokka, USMC. "1st MAW in Korea." Marine Corps Gazette, v. 41, no. 5 (May 1957), pp. 42-47; no. 6 (Jun 1957), pp. 20-26. illus.

   General review of Marine ground and carrier-based aviation in Korea between August 1950 and July 1953.

110. LCdr M. H. Portz, USNR. "Aerial Artillery: The Marines Fly Close Support." Flying, v. 47, no. 6 (Dec 1950), pp. 16-17, +. illus.

   A brief explanation and discussion of the use of air support in Korea.

111. Col J. H. Reinburg, USMCR. "Night Fighter Squadron." Ordnance, v. 49, no. 268 (Jan-Feb 1965), pp. 416-418.

   The story of the development of night CAS at the beginning of the Korean War.

112. Maj Frank Smyth, USMC. "Night Support: a New Weapon." Marine Corps Gazette, v. 35, no. 11 (Nov 1951), pp. 16-21. illus.

   An examination of the employment of CAS at night in the Chosin operation.

113. Col Anthony Standish, USA. "Infantry--Air Support Single Command." United States Army Combat Forces Journal, v. 2, no. 12 (Jul 1952). pp. 31-34. illus.

   The author praises the cooperation that exists between Marine air and ground units while pointing out the lack of such cooperation between the Air Force and the Army.

114. SSgt Robert W. Tallent, USMC. "Tough Team." Leatherneck, v. 34, no. 3 (Mar 1951), pp. 12-15, +. illus.

   Pertains to the cooperation between ground and air units in the Marine withdrawal from the Chosin Reservoir.

115. "Weakness in Air Force." U. S. News & World Report, (3 Nov 1950), pp. 17-19.

   An explanation of why CAS worked for the Marine Corps and not for the Air Force and Army during the first weeks of the war.

116. William Welch. "Leatherneck Air Force." Flying, v. 45, no. 6 (Dec 1949), pp. 22-23, +. illus.

   Short definition on the mission of Marine aviation with emphasis on air support for ground troops.

117. Gerald E. Wheeler. "Naval Aviation in the Korean War." United States Naval Institute Proceedings, v. 83, no. 7 (Jul 1957), pp. 762-777. illus.

   A brief account, largely pictorial, of carrier-based aircraft including the operations of Marine Fighter Squadron (VMF) 323 and 214 aboard USS Badoeng Strait and Sicily, respectively.

118. Sgt Bob Bowen, USMC. "Close Air Support." _Leatherneck_,
      v. 50, no. 5 (May 1967), pp. 22-25. illus.

      Briefly considers the use of CAS in Vietnam.

119. Jonathan Carmen. "OV-10: Versatile Battlefield Aircraft."
      Army, v. 16, no. 11 (Nov 1966), pp. 16, +.

      The article extols the virtues of the OV-10,
      the proposed counterinsurgency aircraft, as a many-
      sided, all-around support aircraft.

120. Maj C. A. Houseman, USMC. "Twin-Boom Bronco Newest Corps
      Aircraft." _Marine Corps Gazette_, v. 52, no. 5
      (May 1968), p. 16. illus.

      A list of the assets of the OV-10A as a
      potential counterinsurgency weapon.

121. Maj E. A. Laning, USMC. "Fly LARA for Proficiency."
      Marine Corps Gazette, v. 48, no. 6 (Jun 1964),
      pp. 30-31.

      Proposal for the Marine Corps to obtain a counter-
      insurgency plane--LARA (Light Armed Reconnaissance
      Aircraft)--to be used in brush fire wars, such as
      Vietnam.

122. MajGen Keith B. McCutcheon, USMC. "Air Support for III
      MAF." _Marine Corps Gazette_, v. 51, no. 8 (Aug 1967),
      pp. 18-23. illus.

      Includes some remarks on the employment of CAS
      in Vietnam.

123. C. M. Plattner. "Marine Control of Air Tested in Combat."
      Aviation Week & Space Technology, v. 84., no. 7
      (14 Feb 1966), pp. 90-91, +. illus.

      A general description of the activities of
      Marine aviation in Vietnam with a capsule view on
      the utilization of CAS.

124. Maj J. W. Rider, USMC, and Capt W. L. Buchanan, USMC.
      "Cobra or Bronco: An Assessment of a Mission."
      Marine Corps Gazette, v. 52, no. 5 (May 1968),
      pp. 36-39. illus.

            Comparison of the limitations and capabilities
      of helicopter gunships (more specifically the AH-16
      with the OV-10A Bronco, a fixed-winged plane) in
      CAS missions.

125. Capt Robert V. Sabia, USMC. "The AO and the Field
      Commander." Marine Corps Gazette, v. 52, no. 5
      (May 1968), pp. 45-49. illus.

            An assessment of the reasons for the inadequacies
      of the Marine aerial observation system in Vietnam
      with recommendation for corrective action.

126. LtCol Allan R. Scholin, ANG. "Close Air Support: How
      it Works Today." The National Guardsman, v. 21,
      no. 3 (Mar 1967), pp. 2-9. illus.

            Primarily, an account of the Air Force and
      Army's version of the employment of CAS in Vietnam
      with a brief mention of the Marine Corps' interpre-
      tation of the doctrine.

127. Col Robert F. Steinkraus, USMC. "Air/Ground Coordination."
      Marine Corps Gazette, v. 50, no. 5 (May 1966),
      pp. 29-31.

            Focuses attention on some of the procedures
      involved in air support in Vietnam.

128. LtCol D. K. Tooker, USMC, et al. "Armed Helicopters."
      Marine Corps Gazette, v. 50, no. 5 (May 1961), pp.
      45-51. illus.

            A discussion by four officers on the use of
      armed helicopters with the conclusion that they
      will never replace fixed wing aircraft but do have
      a place in the air/ground team concept.

129. Cdr Henry Urban, Jr., USN. <u>Close Air Support</u>. Rpt no. 3206. Maxwell Air Force Base, Alabama: Air War College, Air University, 1966. 57 pp.

　　　　Student study dealing basically with the effectiveness of the end product of CAS along with some remarks on the Marine Corps and its development of the doctrine.

130. U. S. Congress. House. Committee on Armed Services. Report of Special Sub-Committee on Tactical Air Support. <u>Close Air Support</u>. Washington, 1966. 15 pp.

　　　　An analysis and comparison by the "Pike Committee" of the doctrine of CAS as utilized by the Air Force and the Marine Corps in the early part of the war.